BUILDING BLOCKS OF ANIMALS AND PLANTS

ANIMAL LIFE CYCLES

Written by Joseph Midthun

Illustrated by Samuel Hiti

WORLD BOOK

a Scott Fetzer company
Chicago

World Book, Inc.
180 North LaSalle Street
Suite 900
Chicago, Illinois 60601
USA

For information about other World Book publications,
visit our website at **www.worldbook.com**
or call **1-800-WORLDBK (967-5325).**
For information about sales to schools and libraries,
call 1-800-975-3250 (United States),
or 1-800-837-5365 (Canada).

Library of Congress Cataloging-in-Publication Data
for this volume has been applied for.

Building Blocks of Animals and Plants
ISBN: 978-0-7166-4616-7 (set, hc.)

Animal Life Cycles
ISBN: 978-0-7166-4618-1 (hc.)

Also available as:
ISBN: 978-0-7166-4626-6 (e-book)

1st printing March 2022

WORLD BOOK STAFF
Executive Committee
President: Geoff Broderick
Vice President, Editorial: Tom Evans
Vice President, Finance: Donald D. Keller
Vice President, Marketing: Jean Lin
Vice President, International Sales:
    Eddy Kisman
Vice President, Technology: Jason Dole
Vice President, Customer Success:
    Jade Lewandowski
Director, Human Resources: Bev Ecker

Editorial
Manager, New Content: Jeff De La Rosa
Associate Manager, New Product:
    Nicholas Kilzer
Sr. Editor: Shawn Brennan
Proofreader: Nathalie Strassheim

Graphics and Design
Sr. Visual Communications Designer:
    Melanie Bender
Sr. Web Designer/Digital Media Developer:
    Matt Carrington
Coordinator, Design Development and
    Production: Brenda B. Tropinski
Book Design: Samuel Hiti

Acknowledgments:
Created by Samuel Hiti and Joseph Midthun
Art by Samuel Hiti
Additional art by David Shephard/
    The Bright Agency
Additional spot art by Shutterstock
Text by Joseph Midthun

TABLE OF CONTENTS

There is a glossary on page 39. Terms defined in the glossary are in type **that looks like this** on their first appearance.

ANIMAL LIFE CYCLES

These stages make up the **life cycle**.

All living things go through different stages as they grow and develop.

Life cycles help us understand how living things change over time.

The whole sequence of changes through which an **organism** passes during its lifetime is called its **life history**.

Even a blue whale, the largest animal ever to have lived on Earth, began life as...

...a tiny **embryo** inside its mother.

This embryo grew and divided until the whale was ready to be born.

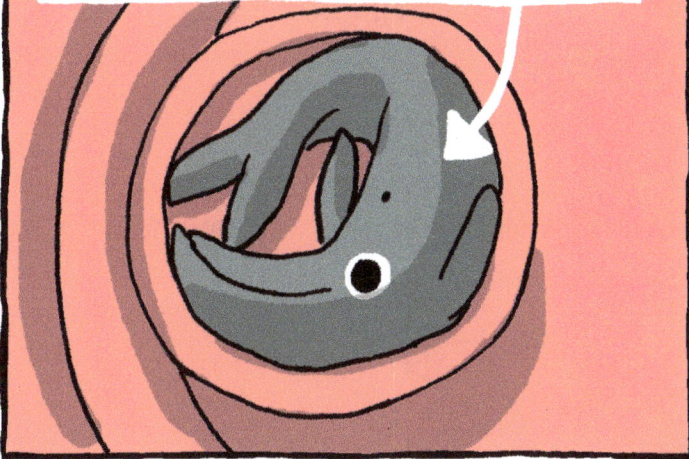

As a baby, the animal depended on its mother for food and protection.

The whale began finding food on its own and grew into an adult.

Finally, it was ready to reproduce, or make another of its kind.

Hi.

Hello.

How an animal lives out its life cycle can have effects on the animal's environment.

At the same time, an animal's environment helps determine whether or not the animal can survive.

FERTILIZATION

Every life cycle begins with **reproduction.**

Reproduction is the creation of **offspring.**

Every kind of living thing reproduces in one way or another.

Many animals reproduce **sexually,** from two parents:

—and a father.

A mother—

sniff sniff

sniff sniff

The male makes special cells for reproduction called **sperm** cells.

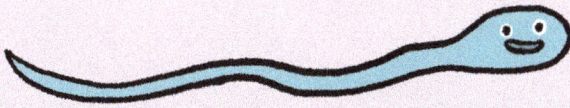

The female makes special reproductive cells called **egg** cells.

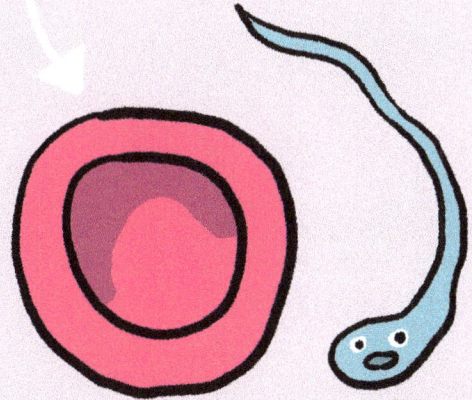

Plants can also reproduce sexually through a process called pollination.

Some plants and animals can reproduce **asexually**, meaning by **themselves**.

Boing

Without reproduction of any kind, living things would die off completely.

Sperm cells and egg cells can join in a process called **fertilization**.

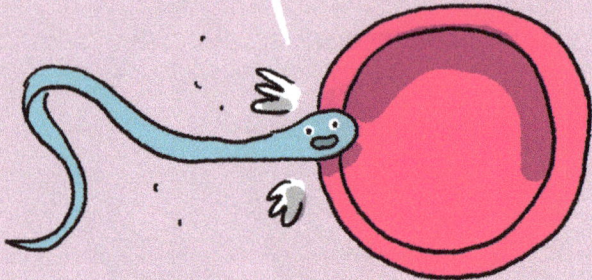

This occurs either inside or outside of the animal's body.

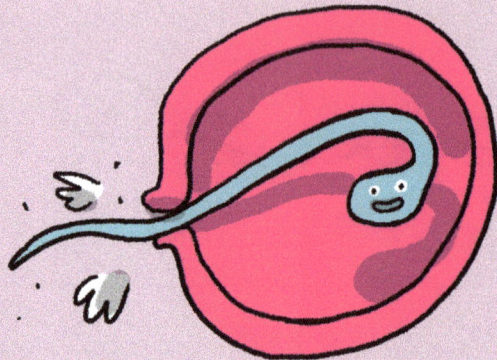

The fertilized egg develops into a new organism.

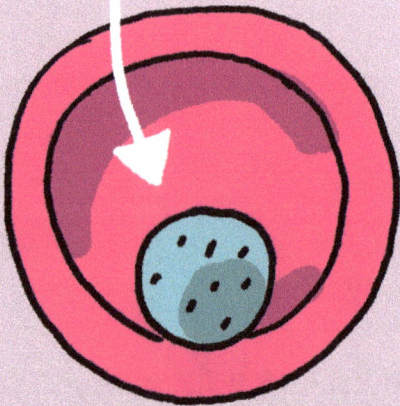

Amphibians, like this newt—

—and fish, like this salmon, can fertilize hundreds of eggs outside of the body.

They produce many eggs because only a few survive to adulthood.

8

Among birds, **mammals**, reptiles, and most animals on land, a few eggs are fertilized inside the female's body.

Because the eggs are protected inside of the female's body, they are more likely to survive and be born.

Plop

However, when this chicken gives birth, it will produce not another chicken—

—but an egg!

Let's take a closer look at some animals that lay eggs containing their offspring.

Pop

EGGS AND OFFSPRING

Similar to how a sunflower seed has the potential to grow into an adult sunflower, an animal egg has the potential to grow into an adult of the same kind of animal.

Both cranes and alligators lay eggs on land.

These types of eggs have tough or leathery shells.

They hold a large amount of nutrients that are contained along with an embryo within a watertight shell.

Both animals' shells also hold in moisture so the eggs will not dry out on land.

The alligator offspring grows inside the shell, developing into a miniature adult, and eventually uses up all of the nutrients.

One day, the offspring is ready to break free from its protective shell.

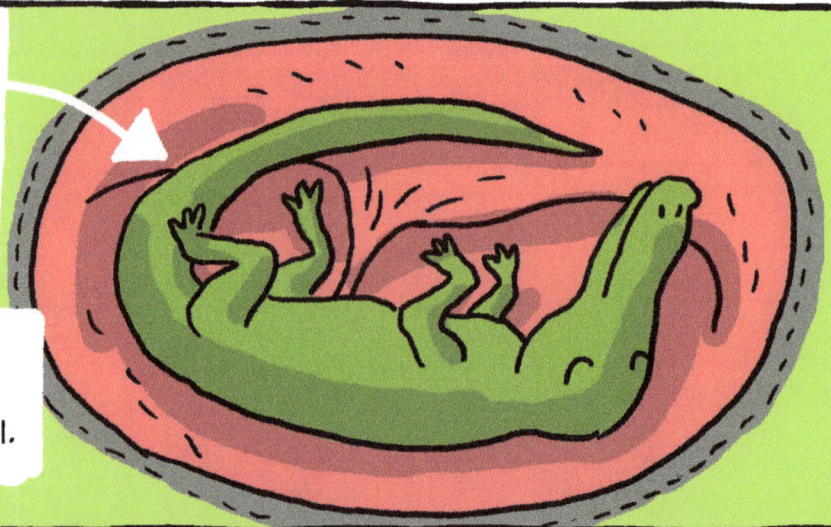

Some baby animals use a tiny hard growth, called an egg tooth, to break their way out.

Eventually, the egg tooth grows out or falls away.

Plop

Amphibians and fish lay their many eggs in the water.

These trout eggs have jellylike coverings but not a hard shell.

The water helps the eggs to stay moist.

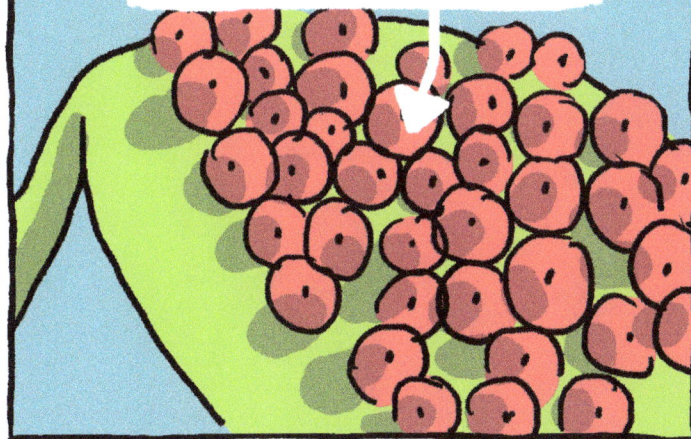

On land, they would dry out and die.

Piff

The eggs of most birds have a similar shape, but vary in color and size.

Most eggs laid in sheltered nests or holes in the ground are white.

Most eggs laid in uncovered nests have protective coloring.

The eggs of this duck are shades of brown.

They blend right in with the cattails and reeds.

Nearly all mammals develop their young from eggs inside of the body.

After a growing period, the mammal gives birth to live offspring.

Mammals such as horses do not give birth for about 11 months.

Their babies, called foals, can walk a few hours after they are born.

The platypus and echidna are both examples of mammals that lay eggs—

Like a bird!

However, after their young hatch, the mothers still feed their babies milk—

Like a mammal!

PARENTAL CARE

Most amphibians, fish, and reptiles provide little or no care for their young.

They usually have many offspring because most will not survive to adulthood.

Are we there yet?

Other animals, like this kangaroo, provide more care.

They usually have fewer offspring because most will survive.

The baby kangaroo, or joey, is carried around in its mother's pouch until it is ready to run and hop on its own.

Most birds sit on top of their eggs to keep them warm.

After the eggs hatch, the parents bring the chicks food, like worms, small insects, or even small mammals, until the chicks can fly.

Many mammals are born helpless.

All mammals care for their young by providing them with milk.

They need care from their parents for months or even years.

You're a mammal—

—look at you!

Humans are cared for and nurtured for many years to learn and grow into responsible adults.

When an animal interacts with its environment, it can change, or grow.

When animals grow, they learn how to survive on their own and develop their adult bodies.

Many animals will grow and develop in different ways.

Some will grow in size and length.

For instance, crabs molt, or shed, their outer shell covering and grow larger adult bodies.

POP

1   2   3   4

Other animals may lose their baby teeth or grow new adult fur.

Hey, I lost a tooth!

Penguin chicks grow thick coats of feathers to keep warm.

That's right!

Cheetahs grow from a cub to an adult by becoming physically stronger.

Cheetah cubs are kept safe by their mothers and learn the skills needed to hunt as an adult.

Many young animals look much like their adult parents.

A puppy looks like an adult dog, except that it is smaller.

Other animals go through incredible changes as they grow up, or mature.

For example, frog eggs will hatch into tadpoles.

Tadpoles are not like adult frogs.

They have gills for breathing underwater and paddlelike tails to propel them around.

Tadpoles go through a remarkable transformation to become adult frogs.

Over time, they lose their gills and develop lungs to breathe on land.

They absorb their tails and grow legs.

This transformation is called **metamorphosis.**

Hop

Amphibians and insects are among the animals that go through metamorphosis.

BUZZ

Uh oh!

waptch

METAMORPHOSIS AND THE BUTTERFLY

A butterfly's life cycle provides another great example of metamorphosis.

An egg is laid, and from it hatches

A larva!

The larva of a butterfly is called a caterpillar.

The larva does little besides eat leaves and grow larger.

When it has become big enough, it is ready for metamorphosis.

Now, the caterpillar becomes a **pupa**.

The pupa does not eat or move around.

It forms a hard outer shell called a **chrysalis**.

The pupa usually attaches its chrysalis in a sheltered spot high up on a tree branch.

Inside the chrysalis, the caterpillar is becoming a butterfly.

crack

When the metamorphosis is complete, the butterfly swells inside the chrysalis until the brittle shell breaks open.

1

2

3

4

Soon, the adult butterfly spreads out its wings and flies away.

If the butterfly successfully lays eggs, the cycle will start all over again!

METAMORPHOSIS AND THE CATERPILLAR WASP

All insects have complex life cycles that involve metamorphosis.

However, some insects require help from other animals or insects to complete their life cycle.

Bzzz

munch munch

Some wasps actually lay their eggs inside other insects, like this caterpillar.

Jab

HEY?!

It's no wonder these wasps are named caterpillar wasps!

Bzzz

The wasp flies away as if nothing has happened, and the caterpillar goes about its business.

All the while, it carries around the unhatched **larvae,** like a living nest.

When they do hatch, the caterpillar slowly dies as the larvae eat and grow.

When large enough, each larva becomes a pupa, using the caterpillar's body to form small cocoons.

When metamorphosis is complete, the adult insects chew their way out of the cocoons...

...and fly away!

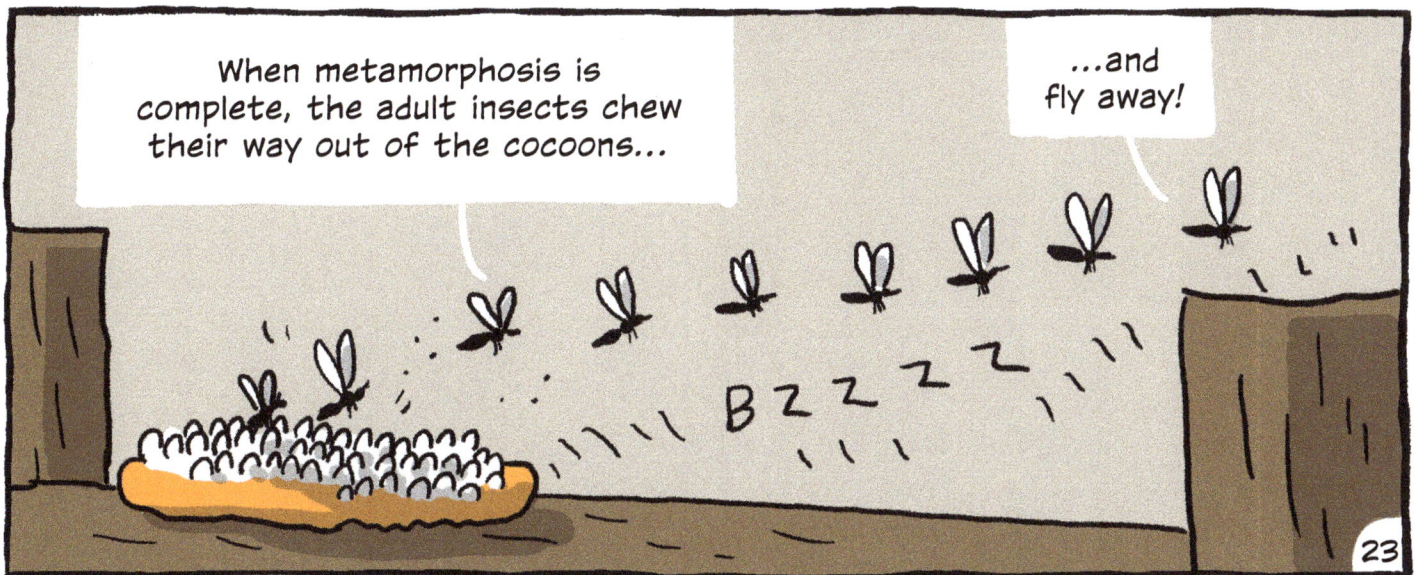

LIFE SPAN

—a measure of how long an animal typically lives in the wild.

All organisms have **life spans**—

Some animals have longer life spans than others.

Some tortoises have lived more than 150 years.

Humans have seen their life expectancy lengthen to upwards of 70 to 80 years.

Huh?

I didn't hear you.

Squirrels may reach 10 years old in the wild.

Eh, sonny?

An adult moth's life span is about one week long.

What?

A mayfly lives for about 24 hours.

You've gotta be kidding me!

In the animal kingdom, a common threat to an animal's life span is **predation**.

BUZZ

Predators are animals that naturally hunt, kill, or eat other animals—

snatch

—their **prey**.

Predator animals are almost always **carnivores**, or meat-eaters.

Prey animals are commonly **herbivores**, or plant-eaters.

?

In the wild, a coyote is a predator.

A hare, if it is not fast enough—

—might be its prey.

When wild animals die much younger than their expected life span, it is called a **life cycle disruption.**

This can happen to any organism, including predators.

Disruptions in animal life cycles can be caused by food shortages, **invasive species,** diseases, habitat destruction, lack of water, pollution, and even tiny **parasites.**

Humans are a direct cause of life cycle disruption in both animals and plants.

As **omnivores,** many humans survive on a balanced diet of animals and plants.

But, humans can also cause indirect disruptions to the organisms in their environment.

Sometimes domesticated, or trained, animals are kept by humans as pets.

Lick Lick

But, sometimes, a pet can be reintroduced into the wild as a stray by escaping or by being abandoned.

Burp

Despite life cycle disruptions, certain jellyfish and other creatures have the ability to grow and change in a way that makes them seem to "live forever."

Hydras are tiny, slender animals that live in ponds and lakes.

These tiny creatures can actually regenerate, or regrow, parts of their bodies.

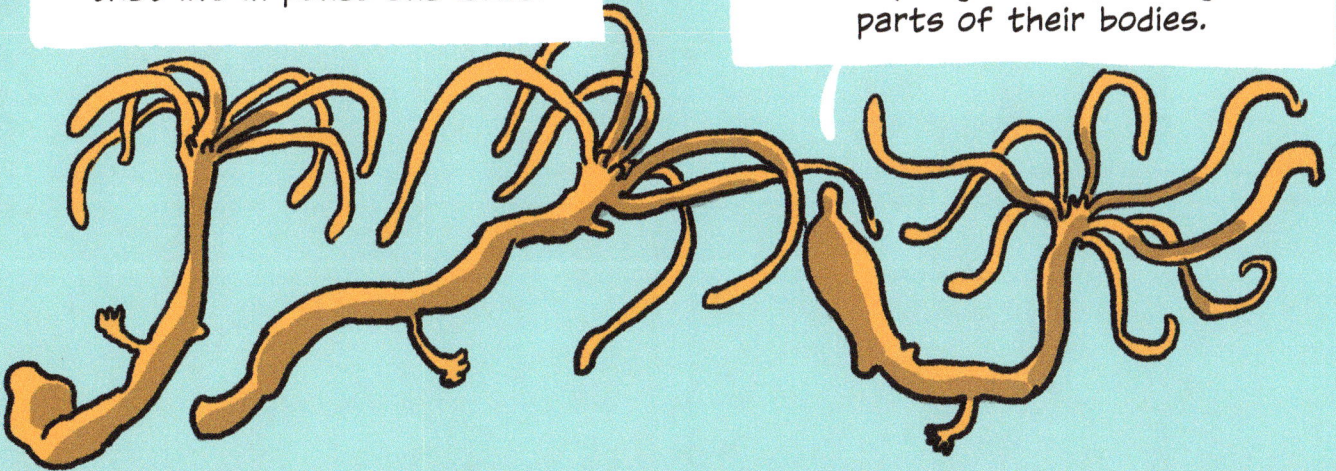

It is estimated that in a period of several weeks, a hydra replaces all of the cells in its body.

The hydra, therefore, never "grows old!"

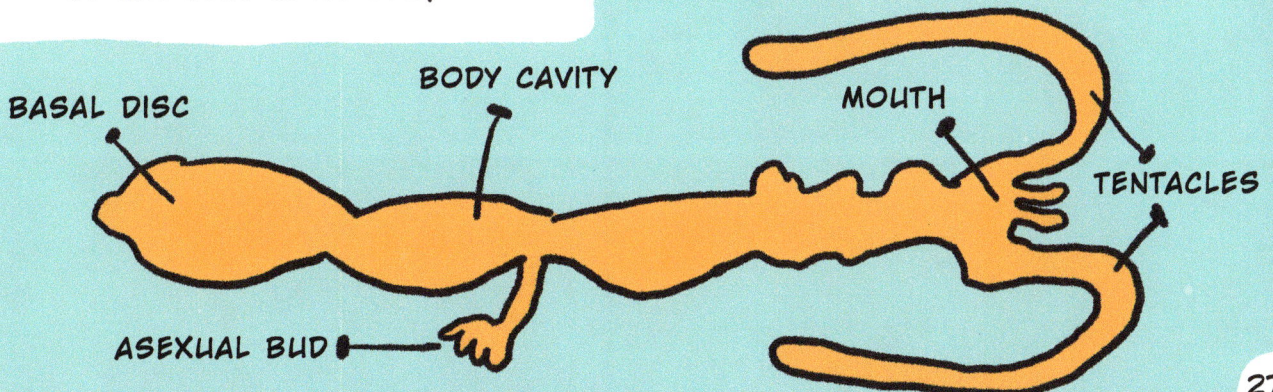

BASAL DISC

BODY CAVITY

MOUTH

TENTACLES

ASEXUAL BUD

THE CIRCLE OF LIFE

All animals are born, grow, and change through interactions with their environment.

And all individual life cycles, for both predators and prey, eventually come to an end.

But at the end, there is a new life cycle beginning.

munch munch

Predator animals eat prey animals to survive.

Prey animals eat plants to survive.

munch munch

And billions of microscopic plants and animals are working just as hard to survive.

So, for every plant and animal death, there are many new lives starting in all kingdoms of life.

Through reproduction and change, animals have thrived on Earth for millions of years.

Each of these individuals has had its own life cycle.

And now, learning about animals and their life cycles has become part of your life cycle!

TIMELINE

Ancient Greek philosopher Aristotle described many aspects of animal development and life.

335 B.C.

Swiss naturalist Maria Sibylla Merian proved that caterpillars undergo metamorphosis to become butterflies.

1677

German scientist Ernst Haeckel stated that the development of an embryo reflects the organism's evolution.

1866

1669

Dutch biologist Jan Swammerdam proved that the larva, pupa, and adult insect were phases in the development of a single individual, not distinct creatures.

1859

French scientist Louis Pasteur demonstrated that organisms do not develop by spontaneous generation.

Plop

Scientists discovered that metamorphosis in frogs is largely controlled by thyroid hormones.

English scientist Charles Elton coined the term *ecology* and described the circle of life.

Scientists identified homeobox genes that control the development of organisms.

1916

1927

1983

1978

1924

German biologist Hans Spemann described how embryos develop in organisms.

German biologist Christiane Nüsslein-Volhard described how genes control the early development of embryos.

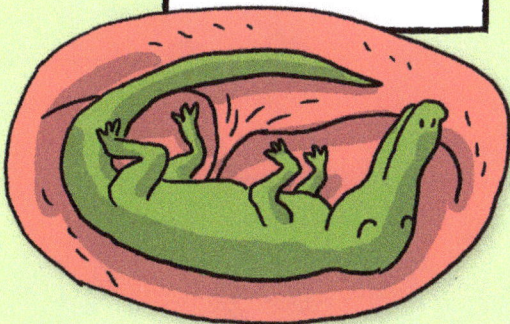

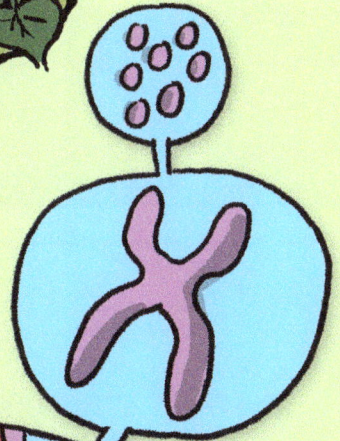

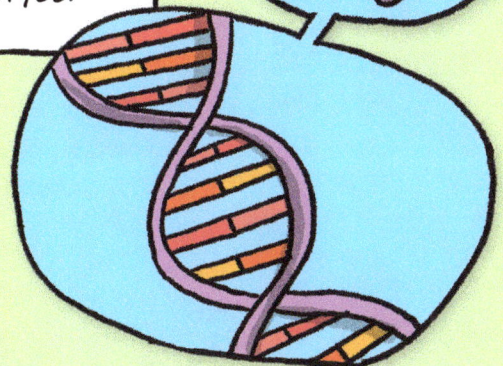

31

WHO'S WHO: MARIA SIBYLLA MERIAN

Hold that pose!

Much of our understanding of the butterfly life cycle and metamorphosis is due to one pioneering scientist.

Maria Sibylla Merian spent many years observing nature. She was especially interested in insects and made hundreds of detailed illustrations.

Maria even raised insects like silkworms with everything they needed to live and reproduce so that she could study their life cycle.

Believe it or not, people used to think that insects grew fully formed out of mud!

My careful observations and illustrations showed that butterflies and other insects have a complex life cycle.

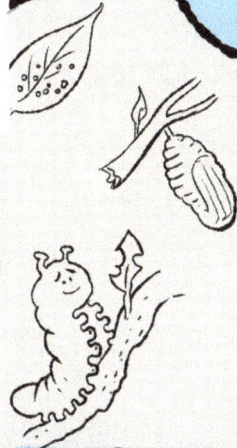

egg

caterpillar

adult butterfly

pupa in chrysalis

In my illustrations, I detailed all of the steps in the metamorphosis of dozens of insects. I proved once and for all that insects did not come fully formed from mud.

Can I move yet?

Fact File

Name: Maria Sibylla Merian

Born: 1647 in Frankfurt, Germany

Occupation: Naturalist and scientific illustrator

Claim to fame: Merian described the life cycles of nearly 200 species of insects and amphibians.

33

CAN YOU BELIEVE IT?!

The mayfly has the **shortest lifespan** of any animal—about 24 hours.

The **Greenland shark** may live up to **400 years or more!**

Sand tiger shark embryos will eat their **own siblings** before they are born!

Elephants carry their young for 18 to 22 months before giving birth— **the longest of any mammal.**

The world's oldest known wild bird, an albatross (seabird) named Wisdom, **hatched an egg at age 70!**

POP

Insects called cicadas may **develop underground for 17 years.**

Once the adults emerge, the adults live only a few weeks to reproduce before they die.

Bowhead whales may live more **than 200 years—** longer than any other mammal.

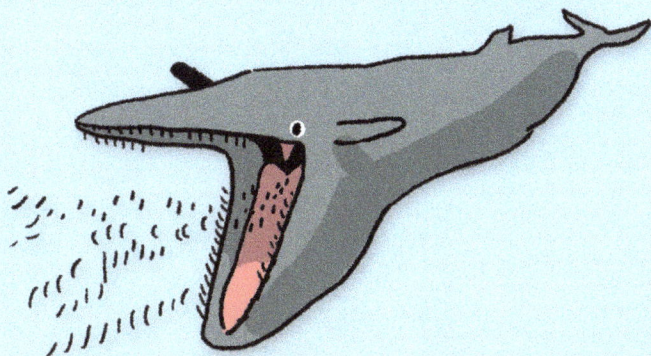

Fish known as *mouthbrooders* carry their eggs in their mouths until they hatch and will often keep their young there well afterward.

Some fish **switch** from being male to female during their life!

35

ACTIVITY:
CALLING ALL BUTTERFLIES!

You can plant a special garden that will attract all kinds of butterflies.

There are more than 10,000 known species of butterflies in the world. Of course, there aren't that many in your neighborhood. But chances are good you can find quite a few different varieties.

First, go to a plant nursery and look for these plants. Caterpillars love to eat these!

Iron Weed

Goldenrod

Butterfly bush

Milkweed

Butterfly weed

Daisy

Phlox

The best time to plant a butterfly garden is in late spring or early summer. Do some research to find other plants that help attract butterflies in your area.

Check on your butterfly garden often. Keep a notebook and record when you see caterpillars and butterflies.

Try to identify the butterflies! How many kinds of butterflies can you see?

WORDS TO KNOW

asexual reproduction the process by which an organism produces an offspring without sperm cells or egg cells.

carnivore an animal that feeds on other animals.

chrysalis the hard outer shell that holds a pupa as it develops into a butterfly.

egg the reproductive cell produced by females.

embryo an animal or human in the early stages of its development, just after fertilization.

fertilization the process by which a male sperm cell and a female egg cell join together.

herbivore an animal that feeds on plants.

invasive species a nonnative species that moves into a new area and replaces the native species.

larva; larvae an active, young form of an animal before it goes through metamorphosis; more than one larva.

life cycle the stages that a living thing goes through as it develops.

life cycle disruption an unexpected shortening of an organism's life span.

life history the sequence of changes through which an organism passes during its lifetime.

life span the measure of how long an organism typically lives in the wild.

mammal a type of animal that has a backbone, grows hair, and feeds its young on the mother's milk.

metamorphosis the transformation of an animal from an immature form to an adult form.

offspring the young of an organism.

omnivore an animal that feeds on plants and other animals.

organism any living thing.

parasite a living thing that benefits at the expense of another organism.

predation when one organism eats another.

predator an animal that hunts and feeds on other animals.

prey an animal that is hunted by other animals for food.

pupa the inactive state of an animal going though metamorphosis.

reproduction the way living things make more of their own kind.

sexual reproduction the process by which organisms produce offspring with sperm cells and egg cells.

sperm the reproductive cell produced by males.

INDEX

POP